Life's Elusive Wisdoms

A Guide to Getting Life Back in Focus

By

M. W. Niles

I hope you Enjoy it

Michael Niles

ISBN: 1-4033-8619-6 (e-book)
ISBN: 1-4033-8620-X (Paperback)
ISBN: 1-4033-8621-8 (RocketBook)

Library of Congress Control Number: 2002095186

This book is printed on acid free paper.

Printed in the United States of America
Bloomington, IN

1stBooks - rev. 10/23/02

Piece by piece taking back control and bringing back into focus the challenges of your life to fully realize the beauty and fulfillment that belongs to you...

M. W. Niles...

M. W. Niles

The attempt to impress other people is a fool's journey; you'll never reach the top of the mountain of all their envies and insecurities

The outer person you see is an
illusion,
A reflection in a pond of what they
wish to be...
The real depth of a person is as the
water below, look there for your
answers.

M. W. Niles

What you do not decide for your self will be decided for you

*Shall you be a victim in this life, or
a victor?
You can decide which to be!*

If you are holding on to that baggage "just in case" you need it, then you are doomed to always need it throughout your life!

Perhaps if you weren't always looking back at the baggage your dragging behind, you wouldn't keep running into posts in front of you.

If you're in search of rewarding solitude, try going the extra mile for someone in life, you're assured to find few others there.

If today's problem won't matter in a year, then why are you not treating it as such?

A person who is petty, bickers and gossips always feeds off of the misery and misfortune of others. They are often the first to offer a shoulder to cry on as they whisper too another.. Be cautious who you confide in.

Bickering and complaining are like weeds in the garden, they will choke out all the flowers and all you'll have left are weeds.

We often say, "we need it"...We always mean we <u>want</u> it, do you recognize your true needs?

When controlling the body its best to start with the tongue, the attitude is sure to follow.

Life is an endless chain of decisions; one is intertwined to the next. . To change the cycle of your life it starts with one solid decision linked to the next.

Often its better to want than to have...
Having is often disappointing.

M. W. Niles

Pride and over-confidence comes before the.. embarrassing apologies.

Those who quarrel all have the same thing in common; they're all armed with the sword of self-righteousness, and the impenetrable shield of rationalizations.

*Stresses in our life is only caused
by our perception of the source*

To win a battle in your life, you must first win the battle with your attitude.

M. W. Niles

To have self-control is to have power over your life

The many struggles in your life
can be overcome,
if the many are overcome one by
one.

If you don't truly know yourself how can you know or understand someone else?

Your worst and most difficult obstacles in life are only your perception of the issues themselves.

*To fail at the beginning just
means you haven't succeeded yet!*

The only difference between
winners and losers is they're
interpretation of the task ahead.

With no perseverance to finish comes no reward.. Have you rewarded yourself lately?

When much is given much is expected...
Beware free gifts.

It takes more than knowing the answer to solve the problem.

To be trusted you must first be trust worthy

Many have answers but few will solve the problems. . Which one do you want to be known for?

To fail once is natural.
To fail twice is human,
And to fail three times.. Is
irresponsible.

To speak first and think later is to regret first and apologize later.

The answers are there only if you want to find them. .But excuses are always readily available.

You are exactly what you have decided yourself to be. . It might be time for some new decisions.

The answers can solve the problems only if your brave enough to use them.

M. W. Niles

Sometimes the hardest word in the English language to pronounce is No, but often the most rewarding.

The correct thing to do is often
the unpopular thing to do.

It is better to openly speak what you feel than to be silently misunderstood.

Doing the right thing always brings admiration with time; no matter how unpopular it was..Doing the "easy" thing has never been praised.

M. W. Niles

Gossip is known to be lies but treated as truth.. How do you treat it?

Isn't it remarkable how those who
are miserable in life can tell you
every time they have been
wronged...
But those who are happy and at
peace can't even remember the last
time they were wronged...
Its your choice what to bring along
with you on this journey.

M. W. Niles

*A false statement said once is
known as a lie, said twice is known
as rumor, said three times is known
to be fact.*

To brag is to show your insecurities for the entire world to see.

M. W. Niles

To assume something without getting the facts is a mistake you may not soon forget.

It's always someone else's fault unless it's something good...
Are you fault finding or praise giving to others?

Only those who dare to be different in this world make a difference in life.. It's often the first step in changing your own.

*Gossip lives only in the present
but truth tells its tale forever.*

M. W. Niles

*You can always obtain
knowledge...Wisdom is knowing
how and when to use it.*

Rumors are unsubstantiated lies;
at least until
you tell someone else, then they
become fact...
Be careful whom you get your facts
from.

Perhaps you won't get in trouble for what you're saying if you weren't always speaking.

We all strive to be an individual
but
all want to be the same.. Are you
a follower?

To seek constant pleasure is to find constant discontent.

*We have so much knowledge
but understand so little.*

Only the fool allows his negative habits to determine his destiny.

It's easier to hear what other
people implying
if you are listening and not
speaking.

If you're waiting for others to set the "good examples", then what examples are you setting? Bad ones?

To say, "do as I say not as I do"
is to force
submission in your presence but
rebellion in your absence.

Perhaps if we said what we truly meant the first time we would not have to repeat ourselves so often.

Anything quickly gained is quickly lost, true happiness is found through time.

M. W. Niles

Anyone can argue for what
they've always believed in. But try
to defend a different point of view.
You may be enlightened by the
outcome.

We all have good ideas but wait for someone else to carry them out.. Are you waiting for someone?

To be indecisive is to have even your closest friends doubt your words and actions.

If you're waiting for the right moment then it's probably already passed you by.

M. W. Niles

An objective without a plan is like a fish out of water, it has no control over its own outcome.

Be careful whom you cheat in life,
in the long run you may have
cheated yourself.

M. W. Niles

To set examples you must use
actions first, and then words are
often un-needed...
Do you speak too much?

Wisdom is seeing someone else's view before your own, and then making the decision.

The quest for knowledge and the quest for understanding often share the same path but not the same destination.

To use the excuse, "if I only had
the time"
is really to say, "If I only had the
time, I would surely waste it
again"

To use compassion without logic is to act as a fool; to use logic without compassion is to act as a tyrant.

The world can be as simple or as complex as you want to perceive it.

M. W. Niles

A fool's dilemma is himself; give him no more credit.

We all use pride to not look as a fool; but in the end its our pride that makes us the fool.

You can accomplish no more physically than your attitude will allow.

*All understanding is achieved
with patience, diligence and
discipline.. Are you in a hurry?*

When all logic fails and no answers are to be found; time reveals all, and time is where all solutions are found.

*To the unknowing the wise are
seen as fools.*

Secrets are best poured slowly to savor every morsel of truth, not gulped down like gossip.

A logical man's dilemma is his misunderstanding.

M. W. Niles

People will always know something of you; you decide whether it's good or bad.

Logic can sometimes rob you of the happiness of a spring day or the beauty and peacefulness that's all around you.. Logic only knows step one step two step three...

M. W. Niles

*Instant overwhelming feelings
and emotions are like a title wave;
once they pass what you have left is
often a mess to clean up.*

The body's largest obstacle is the mouth.. Have you tamed your obstacle?

To conduct yourself with honesty, integrity and self respect means not hurting and in turn saying I'm sorry to the ones you love, if not for you, for them.

To give is to gain popularity.. To borrow is to find out who your true friends really are.

To want something so much that you would do anything to have it, is the first steps to acquiring it in all the wrong ways.

If a secret is to become like fine wine then its best kept locked away in a dark place and aged… Released to soon and all you have is juicy gossip.

M. W. Niles

To love someone is to be able to let go if needed.. Letting go is often needed to be able to keep someone... It's the difference between selfless love and selfish love.

There is no such thing as a true secret, just something everyone doesn't know yet.

The treacherous are at constant
conflict with the innocent,
scheming, plotting, lying and
cheating...
The innocent are often unaware of
the battle until there are wounded.

Happiness is not measured at the moment, but by the things that will bring it over time.

M. W. Niles

*Too much freedom could spell the
end for all freedoms.*

If you have to soul search and ask others to determine if you have truly been wronged by another, then chances are you have wronged yourself by collecting baggage for the trip down the road your headed...
Let it go, there are nicer trips in life to take.

Enormous pressures and heat create
a beautiful and unbreakable
diamond...
Love is formed the same way,
strengthened by pressures, tempered
and tested by fire to create a
beautiful and unbreakable bond.

*To win an argument no matter
what the cost with a loved one could
cost you everything in the end...
Are you willing to pay the
admission price for loneliness?*

To not speak out against something you do not agree with is to agree with it.

Don't look so hard; it will be easier to find what it is your searching for.

To mix reality with too much ideal is a dangerous path, only leading to disparity.

For the innocent to overcome the treacherous, they must not give in to the temptation of bitterness and resentment...
These are the things that rob us of all our strengths.

M. W. Niles

Perfection has many definitions but the truest one is Fantasy... Leading only to emotional self-destruction...Don't chase fantasies.

Kindness is learned...
Maliciousness comes naturally.

M. W. Niles

_Cul_tural propaganda is always
known to be fact by its
follower's. History is littered with
"facts" that have become fiction.

The most desired substance in the
world is power...
Its always more desirable to set
standards than it is to live up to
them yourself.

Be mindful not to confuse your reasons with your rationalizations.

If you believe your voice will never make a difference, then it never will.

When you draw a moral line in the sand not to be crossed, its important to know which side of the line you are on at all times.

Conflicts are always fought on excuses rather than reasons.

Every reason has a hidden excuse...
Do you know yours?

Do not be intimidated or offended by someone who is boastful and brags, just take comfort in knowing that he has many problems that he's attempting to hide.

*The outcome is already determined
by the your attitude before you ever
start.*

What you need has always been attainable, if you weren't always chasing what you wanted.

Life is nothing more than an endless chain of decisions.. Are your decisions based on old habits?

Every great accomplishment in history all share the one common link.. They all were created by those who ignored other peoples opinions and ridicule.

M. W. Niles

Attitude is the key that unlocks the doors of happiness and success.

To not admit a problem to yourself
is the pitfall that leads to long and
winding dead ends in roads of
life...
Do you have the time for such
pointless delays on this trip?

Purpose in life is not found in how others can benefit you but <u>true</u> purpose in life is found in the benefits you can bring to other lives.

*Positive attitudes bring about
positive results…
Negative attitudes always end in
negative results.*

Always ask yourself, "Does this issue deserve this much attention, consideration and concern?" If not then why are you punishing yourself?

Have you stopped and counted all
the wonderful things in your life
lately? Or were you too busy
thinking about all the bad ones?

Effort spent is accomplishment gained.. And even patience is an effort.

Be cautious about taking to heart venomous remarks or opinions of others.. Be weary of allowing their bitterness to influence your decisions or destiny.

Your life will change the moment you stop wishing your life were different and just make it different.

About the Author

Michael takes a simple, strait forward approach to solving life's problems.

Often proud to say "I don't follow modern psycho babble"

He has dedicated his life to studying the human condition and studied many different philosophies and religions. Michael is a true student of people. He has a natural gift for seeing directly into the root of the issue.

If you're looking for a guidebook to help ease you through some troubling moments, then Life's Elusive Wisdoms gives you over a hundred tips on how to bring your life back into focus.

Printed in the United States
909600001B

9 781403 386205